A United Kingdom
1500–1750

John D Clare

Contents

Nelson

A TUDOR MONARCH

Henry VIII in 1516

Henry VIII became king of England in 1509. What was he like?

A description by the ambassador from Venice

His majesty is the most handsome prince I ever saw.
He is taller than usual, with a very strong calf to his leg.
His face is very fair and bright, and he has auburn hair – which he
combs straight and short in the French fashion. His round face is so
5 beautiful that it would suit a pretty woman, although his throat is
rather long and thick.

He was born on 28 June 1491, so he will be 25 the month after next.

He speaks French, English and Latin, and a little Italian. He plays well
on the lute and the harpsichord, and sings from music at sight. He is
10 a better archer than any man in England, and he jousts marvellously.

I tell you – he is in every way a most talented prince.

Report of the Venetian ambassador (1516)

calf: *back of the leg between the knee and the ankle.*
auburn: *light ginger.*
lute: *a musical instrument like a guitar.*
15 **harpsichord**: *a musical instrument like a piano.*
sings from music at sight: *Henry could read music and sing tunes he had
    never heard before.*
jousts: *fights on horseback, using lances, at a tournament.*

Right: a portrait of Henry VIII painted in 1536 by
Hans Holbein, a court painter.

3

Katherine's Story

Love

*In 1501 a young girl of 15 sailed to
England from Spain. She was going to
marry Arthur Tudor, the Prince of Wales.
Her name was Katherine of Aragon.*

5 Katherine was not happy. England
seemed very cold and damp. Her priest
was a rude, noisy man; her maid bullied
her. Arthur was pale and ill. He had a
terrible cough. She much preferred
10 Arthur's brother, Henry – he was strong,
handsome, and a good dancer.

However, Katherine had to marry
Arthur. They went to live in Wales. Just
five months later, Arthur died.

15 Katherine did not go home to Spain.
She was told that she must now marry
Henry. When Henry became king in
1509, they had a magnificent wedding.

At first, they were very happy. Henry
20 took her to jousts and feasts. To prove
his friendship with the king of France,
Henry had said that he would never
shave off his beard. When he found out
that Katherine did not like beards,
25 Henry shaved it off. It almost caused
a war!

Marriage

*By 1525 the marriage between Henry and
Katherine had grown cold.
It had grown cold for two reasons.*

One reason was that Henry wanted a 30
son who would be king after him. But
Katherine's first child was a girl who
died at birth. Then she had a son who
died when he was seven weeks old. In
all, Katherine became pregnant 17 times, 35
but only one child lived – a daughter
called Mary. By 1525 Katherine was too
old to have any more children.

The second reason was that Henry had
met a young girl called Anne Boleyn. 40
Anne had just come back to England
from France. She had beautiful black
hair and eyes. She wore the latest
fashions, and looked good in green
(her favourite colour). She was just 45
18 years old.

Henry VIII jousting (left), watched by Katherine
and her ladies-in-waiting.

4

However, when Henry tried to flirt
50 with Anne, she ignored him. He carved
her name on trees. He wrote love letters
to her. Anne told him that she would
only love him if he married her.

Henry told Katherine that he wanted
55 to divorce her. She refused. She told him
that she was his true wife, and always
would be.

Then she turned and walked out. Her
ladies-in-waiting cheered.

Divorce

60 *Thomas Wolsey was Henry's Chancellor;*
he looked after government business for
Henry. In 1527, Henry told Wolsey to
ask the Pope — the head of the Roman
Catholic Church — to grant a divorce. But
65 *the Pope said 'No'.*

Katherine had a nephew called Charles.
Charles was the ruler of Germany,
Holland, Italy and Spain. In 1527 he
had captured Rome. Pope Clement was
70 scared of Charles. He did not dare to
give Henry a divorce.

Henry was angry. He sent for
Wolsey to stand trial. Wolsey thought
he was going to be executed. He died
on the way to London. Some people   75
said Wolsey died of fright.

Then Henry talked to two men:
Thomas Cromwell and Thomas
Cranmer.

Thomas   80
Cromwell, a
lawyer (who
became
Chancellor).

Thomas   85
Cranmer, a
priest (who
became
Archbishop of
Canterbury).   90

Cromwell and Cranmer told Henry to
break away from the Pope, and make
himself Head of the Church in England.
If Henry did this, they said, he could
give himself a divorce.   95

That is what Henry did. He passed the
Act of Supremacy, which said he was
Supreme Head of the Church in
England. He married Anne in 1533, and
divorced Katherine.   100

5

The Dissolution

After Henry had made himself Supreme Head of the Church, he decided to close down the monasteries. This is called the 'dissolution' of the monasteries.

5 There were many reasons for this. All priests and monks had promised to obey the Pope, so Henry was afraid that he would not be able to rely on their loyalty. It was also true that the
10 monasteries were becoming out of date. In the Middle Ages, monks had been very useful. They had copied books, taught children, cared for the sick, sheltered travellers, and given money to
15 the poor. But times had changed. The printing press had been invented. There were more schools, hospitals and inns. Most people no longer needed the monasteries.

20 Also, for centuries, people had given land and money to the monasteries, hoping that this would earn them a place in heaven. The Church owned one quarter of all the land in England.
25 The monasteries had great wealth. One modern historian thinks:

> . . . this was probably Henry's main reason for closing the monasteries.
> **Peter Moss**, *History Alive I (1968)*

30 In 1535, Henry told Thomas Cromwell to arrange a report on the monasteries. It was called the *Valor Ecclesiasticus* (meaning 'what the Church is worth').

Two of the monks who were executed
35 for refusing to swear that Henry was Head of the Church.
Notice the beggar; because the monasteries have closed he has nowhere to go for food or money.

Monks and nuns were supposed to be 40 poor. They had promised to spend their lives working and praying. They were not supposed to have sexual relations. But the *Valor Ecclesiasticus* included many reports about places where monks and 45 nuns behaved badly (see sources 1-4). Peter Moss writes:

> Cases like this were not frequent . . . but they gave Henry an excuse.

Between 1536 and 1539, Henry closed 50 down nearly 825 monasteries and nunneries. He took their wealth. Henry became the richest king in Europe.

Ten thousand monks and nuns were made homeless. Monks were not badly 55 treated. Most became village priests. Nuns were less well treated. They could not become priests, and they were given only a robe. Many were forced to become servants or beggars. 60

1 Peterborough Monastery

The lord abbot does not choose
studious monks but looks for lazy ones.
There is a tavern where the brothers drink
in bad weather . . . .

The sacrist of the monastery has in his bedroom
secretly a certain maiden named Joan Turner.

2 Bury St Edmunds Monastery

The abbot loved to play dice and spent
much on it. He did not preach in public.
There was a frequent coming and going of
women to the monastery.

3 Ramsey Monastery

Many of the monks devote themselves
to hunting and other sports . . . . The
dormitory is so neglected that rain falls on
the brothers' beds . . . . The prior is frequently
drunk.

4 Glastonbury Abbey

When the abbot's answers were not to
our purpose we . . . searched his study
and found . . . a written book against the
divorce of the King.

5 Bury St Edmunds Nunnery

I could not find out
anything bad about the
nunnery no matter how hard
I tried.

I believe everybody had got
together and agreed to keep
things secret.

Sources 1–5 are reports by
the inspectors who Thomas
Cromwell sent to the
monasteries and nunneries in
1535. He told the inspectors to
go also to the local inns, to
collect gossip about the monks
and nuns.

QUESTIONS

1 Find four reasons why the
monasteries were closed
down and explain them in
your own words.

2 Make a list of ten faults
that the inspectors found in
sources 1–4.

3 Peter Moss thinks the
monasteries were closed
because Henry wanted
their wealth, and that the
monks' behaviour was just
an excuse. Use source 5
and your own knowledge
to say whether or not you
agree.

Below: Ruins such as these at
Rievaulx in Yorkshire show how
wealthy the monasteries were.

The Pilgrimage of Grace

1 In 1536, the peasants of Lincolnshire rebelled.

MONASTERIES CLOSED! A TAX ON BAPTISMS! A TAX ON BREAD!

They killed two tax collectors. One they hanged. The other they sewed into the skin of an ox and set their dogs on him.

2 They asked a Yorkshireman called Robert Aske to be their leader.

5 But some pilgrims were saying that Henry was 'the Mole' – an evil king prophesied in old legends.

6 Also, the pilgrimage was joined by nobles – including the powerful Lord Percy. Many nobles hated 'low-born' Cromwell, whom they nicknamed 'Crumb'.

MUCH TROUBLE COMES FROM A CRUMB STUCK IN THE THROAT!

9 Henry was furious.

I MARVEL THAT IGNORANT PEOPLE WILL INSTRUCT US WHAT THE RIGHT FAITH SHOULD BE.

10 The royal army marched north.

However, it had only 7,000 soldiers. Henry's army did not attack the pilgrims.

3 From Yorkshire and County Durham, 30,000 peasants rushed to join Aske.

4 Aske gave orders for a peaceful demonstration – a pilgrimage.

The pilgrims carried bread and wine from the Mass, and a banner showing Christ's wounds. They asked Henry to spare the monasteries.

7 On 16 October 1536, the pilgrims captured York.

8 Lord Darcy surrendered Pontefract Castle to the pilgrims.

He said it was because the rebels had captured his grandchildren, but he hated Henry's changes in the Church.

11 Henry offered the pilgrims a free pardon. He promised to think about their demands.

The pilgrims swore loyalty to the king and went home.

12 But Henry ordered 'dreadful execution to be done'.

Aske and 200 pilgrims were executed, along with Lord Darcy and some monks who had joined the rebellion.

Henry's Wives

Anne Boleyn *(born 1507, executed 1536)*
In January 1533 – before he had divorced Katherine of Aragon – Henry married Anne Boleyn. On 1 June 1533, she was crowned queen in Westminster Abbey in London.

Many people hated Anne. One man yelled out: 'God save Queen Katherine!' and another man shouted: 'Goggle-eyed monster.' Henry and Anne's initials – 'H' and 'A' – were on all the carpets and banners. The crowds laughed at them, shouting 'Ha! Ha!'

In 1533 Anne had her first child, a girl called Elizabeth. Henry was furious and refused to go to the baptism.

People also noticed that Anne was becoming more aggressive every day, shouting at Henry and telling him off. Henry started spending time with Jane Seymour, one of Anne's ladies-in-waiting. That made Anne more angry!

Then in 1536 Anne had a miscarriage. She had failed to give Henry a son. Henry told Thomas Cromwell he wanted to get rid of her.

Anne was sent to the Tower of London and put on trial. She was accused of taking other men as lovers – including the king's best friend, her musician (who confessed under torture), her brother, and 'a hundred other men'. It was claimed that she had plotted to kill Henry and take the throne.

On 19 May 1536 Anne was executed on Tower Green. She wore a grey robe trimmed with fur. Reports said that she had a 'goodly, smiling face'.

Anne even admitted that she was guilty. She said: 'I pray God, save the king . . . there never was a gentler, or a more merciful prince.'

Henry had brought from France an expert swordsman, who cut off her head with one blow. But Henry did not see Anne die; he was singing love songs to Jane Seymour. That day they announced their engagement.

Queen Anne Boleyn, painted by an unknown artist.

??? QUESTIONS ???

1 Look at the accusations made against Anne. Do you believe them?
2 Why did Anne say *nice* things about Henry at her execution?

50 **Jane Seymour**
*(born 1509,
died 1537)*
Ten days after
Anne Boleyn's
55 execution,
Henry married
Jane Seymour –
in her bedroom!
Jane was quiet
60 and gentle.
Henry always
said that he
loved her more
than any of his
65 other wives. In
1537 she became pregnant, but had problems
having the baby. There were rumours that Henry
told the doctors to 'tear the child from the
womb'.
70 Jane got a fever. The doctors kept her freezing
cold. They put leeches all over her to take away
'bad blood'.
But Henry rejoiced, for the baby was a boy. He
called the child Edward, and held a great baptism
75 party. Twelve days later, Henry's 'favourite wife'
died while he feasted.

Catherine Howard 105
*(born 1521,
executed 1542)*
By this time,
Henry was having
problems at 110
home. The
people had
begun to hate
him. They were
calling him 'a 115
beast and worse
than a beast'. There
were riots and plots.
Needing support, in July
1540 Henry married 120
Catherine Howard. She was the niece of the
powerful Duke of Norfolk. Catherine was 19,
short, plump and very attractive. She was a good
nurse and dressed the large open sores on
Henry's legs. 125
But Catherine found Henry boring. She had love
affairs with other men, including her secretary
and one of Henry's advisers. When he found out,
Henry burst into tears. Then he executed her.

**Anna of
Cleves** *(born
1515, died
80 1557)*
Within hours of
Jane's death,
Henry was
trying to find a
85 fourth wife.
Henry's two
enemies
(Charles V of
Spain and
90 Francis I of
France) had
joined forces to
destroy him.
Henry needed an ally – a country which would be
95 his friend.
On Thomas Cromwell's advice, Henry chose
Anna of Cleves (Cleves was a country in North
Germany). He had seen a portrait of her, painted
by Hans Holbein, but when she arrived Henry did
100 not like her. Anna was plain and fat. She had a
long nose. She could not speak English and sang
out of tune! Henry married Anna in January 1540,
but divorced her six months later. Then he
executed Cromwell.

**Catherine 130
Parr** *(born
1512, died
1548)*
In 1543 Henry
married his last 135
wife. At 31,
Catherine Parr
was older than
Henry's other
wives. She was 140
educated and
gentle. She took
care of his
rotting body and
ruled the country 145
when he was too
ill to cope. She treated Mary, Elizabeth and
Edward as if they were her own children. She
made them into a happy family.
On 28 January 1547, Henry died. He asked to 150
be buried with Jane Seymour. 'A wonderful man,'
said the French ambassador.

EVERYDAY LIFE

The British Isles in 1500

Henry VIII did not control the whole of the British Isles. He did not even fully control the whole of England!

Henry VIII united Wales and England in 1536. But it was not until 1707 that an Act of Union combined Scotland and England into what was called the 'United Kingdom', and Ireland did not become part of the United Kingdom until 1801.

Scotland

In 1500, Scotland was an independent country with its own royal family (the Stuarts) and its own parliament. About 20,000 people lived in Edinburgh, the capital, but the entire population of the country was less than one million. In the north of Scotland – the Highlands – the clans were ruled by their own 'lairds'.

Scotland had a close friendship with France – the 'old alliance' – and there were often wars between England and Scotland. The Scots invaded England in 1496, 1497, 1513, 1522 and 1557. English armies raided Scotland in 1523, 1542, 1544, 1545, 1547 and 1548.

In 1603, after the death of Queen Elizabeth I, King James VI of Scotland became also King James I of England, so the two countries had the same king.

Ireland

In 1500, the population of Ireland was about 1.5 million. Dublin, the main city, had only about 5,000 inhabitants.

The only part of Ireland fully ruled by England was an area around Dublin called the Pale. Most of Ireland was controlled by Irish lords, who ruled as they liked.

Henry VIII began to bring Ireland more under control. Ireland was divided into counties, and made to obey English laws.

Queen Elizabeth I and King James I went further. They took land from the Irish and gave it to English and Scottish 'planters'. These gifts of land were called plantations.

The Irish were Catholics. They hated the plantations. They rebelled in 1562–67, 1569–73, 1579–80, 1594–96 and 1598–1603. The Irish often had help from Spain.

IRELAND

Wales

Population in 1500: a quarter of a million people.
Capital: Cardiff (1,000 inhabitants).

The west of Wales – the Principality – had become part of England in 1284. The rest of Wales, however, was controlled by the Marcher lords, who had great power.

In 1536, Henry VIII passed the Act of Union with Wales. Wales was divided into counties, and had to obey English laws. The Welsh sent MPs to the English Parliament, but English became the official language of the country.

In 1543, a Council of Wales was set up to control the region.

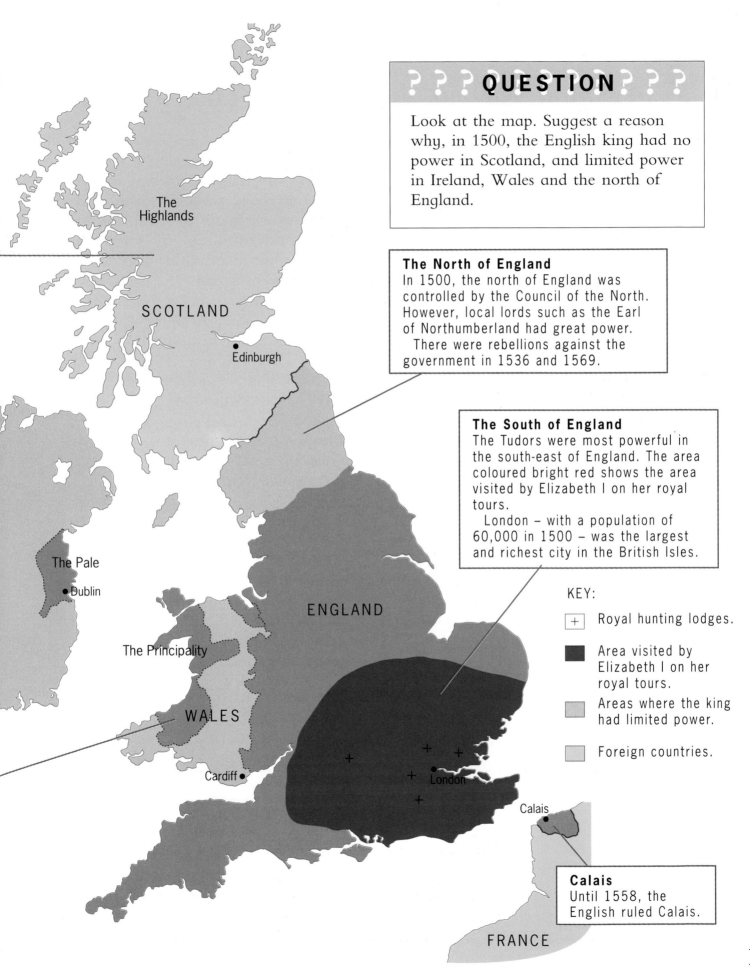

QUESTION

Look at the map. Suggest a reason why, in 1500, the English king had no power in Scotland, and limited power in Ireland, Wales and the north of England.

The Highlands

SCOTLAND

Edinburgh

The North of England
In 1500, the north of England was controlled by the Council of the North. However, local lords such as the Earl of Northumberland had great power.
There were rebellions against the government in 1536 and 1569.

The South of England
The Tudors were most powerful in the south-east of England. The area coloured bright red shows the area visited by Elizabeth I on her royal tours.
London – with a population of 60,000 in 1500 – was the largest and richest city in the British Isles.

The Pale

Dublin

ENGLAND

The Principality

WALES

Cardiff

London

Calais

KEY:

⊞ Royal hunting lodges.

▓ Area visited by Elizabeth I on her royal tours.

▓ Areas where the king had limited power.

▢ Foreign countries.

Calais
Until 1558, the English ruled Calais.

FRANCE

13

London Life in the Time of Henry VIII

A man called John Smith and two women went into a tavern (a pub) near St Bride's Church in London. They were waiting to be served when a crowd of people came in, led by William Kyng, an apprentice. Kyng called for some wine, and he and his friends were served.

At this, Smith rose out of his seat, and went over to William Kyng, saying, 'Thou whoreson, why takest thou my wine?' When Kyng protested that it was his own wine, Smith 'out of cruel evil took the said pot of wine and hit the aforesaid William on the head'. He also took his dagger out. The other customers stopped the fight, and sent Kyng and his friends away.

Kyng went to another tavern, called The Standard, with two friends. One of them saw a man and shouted, 'Yonder goes he that hit thee in the tavern.' In fact, he had made a mistake. It was not John Smith. It was a law student called Oystreche, from Clifford's Inn (one of the law schools near London).

Kyng and his friends stopped Oystreche, who seemed confused. 'I know thee not, nor yet did I hit thee,' he said. Kyng hit Oystreche, who ran to a nearby house. The people who lived there stopped the fight. Kyng realised he had attacked the wrong man. He said he was sorry.

Sorry, however, was not good enough for Oystreche. He went back to Clifford's Inn and collected a crowd of his friends. They went down into London to complain to Kyng's master. Kyng's master said he was sorry and that he would deal with the matter, and everyone went home.

Everyone, that is, except two young law students. They took some weapons and hid in 'an alley going down to the river by Fleet Bridge'. They planned to ambush William Kyng. Instead, in another case of mistaken identity, they attacked one John Penyngton – a bow-and-arrow maker – who was innocently making his way home. Penyngton screamed for help. The attackers were arrested and taken to the constable.

When the students at Clifford's Inn heard what had happened, they put on their 'armour with axes and long and short swords'. Then they swarmed back into London to rescue their friends. The men of St Bride's formed a gang and drove them back after a fierce battle.

The constable was too scared to arrest anyone, and the matter was forgotten.

? ? ? QUESTIONS ? ? ?

1 What does the story tell us about life in London in Tudor times?
2 What can we learn from the pictures of street characters about life in London in Tudor times?

Street Characters

2   Water-seller.

3   Rich merchant and noblewoman.

1   Rat-catcher.

4   Ballad-seller (a sign that some people can read).

8   Town crier, shouting 'Oyez, oyez, oyez!' as he makes public announcements.

5   Watchman.

6   Countrywomen, in town to sell fish.

7   Apprentice boy.

9   Peddler – a travelling shop!

15

Scenes from Town Life

Imagine you had to spend a day in sixteenth-century London. The pictures on pages 16–19 show some of the sights you might expect to see.

? ? ? QUESTION ? ? ?

What sort of information about life in the streets of Tudor and Stuart London cannot be obtained from these pictures?

1 Going into London; the gateway to London Bridge. Note the heads of traitors on poles.

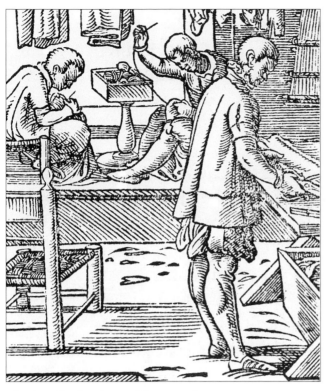

2 A tailor's shop. Why are the men sewing by the shop window?

3 Washerwomen at work.

4 Doing the shopping.

5 In a leather-workers' shop. Note that the shop opens directly onto the street.

6 An Elizabethan fire engine. Can you work out how it worked?

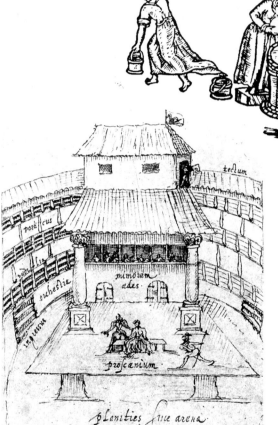

7 The Globe Theatre. This is where Shakespeare's plays were performed.

8 A typical street scene. List everything that made this street an unhealthy place in which to live.

9 A funeral procession.

10 An open-air sermon at
St Paul's Cross.

The Poor

In the sixteenth century many people lived in a state of poverty that we find almost impossible to imagine.

1 A servant's will

Pan and dubbler to Agnes Stevenson.
2 yards of black cloth to Elizabeth Robinson,
whereof I purposed to have made me a gown.
The rest I do whollye give unto John Robinson my master.

Her possessions:

A brasse potte and panne and two pewter dubblers.	9s
Of lynnen, 2 worne codwaynes, a rayle, a chirecheife, smock and a towel.	2s 9d
2 yards of black cloth which should have been her coat.	8s 8d
2 old worne coats.	3s 4d
An hatte, and an old bedde coverlet.	3s 4d

*Will of **Margerye Brankingham** of County Durham, 1573.
Margerye Brankingham was not a beggar
but this was ALL she owned.*

dubbler: *a spoon.*
codwayne: *a kind of shoe.*
rayle: *a nightdress.*

There was no Welfare State or Social Security. People who could not earn enough to support themselves were forced to beg. In 1598, the government passed a Poor Law. Local churches were told to appoint 'overseers' to look after the poor. The area looked after by each church was called a parish.

- *The Impotent Poor* (helpless people such as the old and blind) were to be paid a small amount of money by the parish, or given a licence to beg.
- *The Poor by Casualty* (such as wounded soldiers and sick people) were to be put in the parish workhouse.
- *The Idle Poor* (or 'sturdy beggars') were to be whipped or hanged.

The sources on page 21 will tell you more about people's attitudes to the poor in Tudor times.

2 Tudor beggars

In 1592, Thomas Harman published *A Warning for Vagabonds*, about fake beggars who would trick you out of your money.

The picture on the right shows:
- *Bright Nicholas*, who pretended to be an 'upright gentleman' down on his luck.
- *A soap eater*, who ate soap to make himself froth at the mouth as if he had epilepsy.

Other kinds of sturdy beggars included:
- *Tom O'Bedlam* (pretended to be mad).
- *Whipjacks* (pretended to be old sailors).
- *Drummerers* (pretended to be deaf).

3 The trouble with beggars

This year there assembled 80 rogues who stole a whole load of cheese . . . .

I say that the large numbers of idle, wandering people and robbers are the chief cause of the food shortage, for they do not work but lie idly in ale-houses day and night, eating and drinking too much . . . .

And when they are put in jail, the poor country people they robbed are forced to feed them.

Letter from **Edward Hext**, *1596.*
Edward Hext was a Justice of the Peace.
1596 was a time of famine in England.

4 Two beggar-girls

Alice and Elizabeth Pickering, wandering children, were whipped according to the law, and sent with a pass to Shrewsbury, the place where they were born.

Register of the Parish of Newtimber, 1615

5 Sturdy beggars were whipped through the streets. Sometimes they were chained to a cart. In the background looms the gallows, for persistent offenders.

Birth

The sources on these two pages will give you some information about childbirth in Tudor and Stuart times.

1 My God and my Lord, my defender and protector, I most humbly give you my thanks for Thy mercy . . . and my safe delivery from the pain and peril of childbirth.

A prayer written by **Elizabeth Mordaunt** *after the birth of her son John in 1659.*

2 I was at ease, but now God has broken me apart and shaken me to pieces.

Sir William Brownlow, *writing after the death of his fifteenth child, at the age of nine months.*
Sir William's first son was born in June 1626, but died four months later. He had 18 more children during the next 22 years; only two sons and four daughters survived.

3 Sir Richard Saltonstall brings his children to say goodbye to their mother, who is dying after the birth of the baby. She points to the children, giving him the responsibility of looking after them. This picture was painted c. 1637.

4   Having a baby in Tudor times.

Upbringing

The sources on these two pages will give you some information about how Tudor and Stuart parents brought up their children.

1 Bringing up baby

I would allow no swearing, or speaking of gossip in this home . . . . She must be called by her Christian name, without 'Miss' or
5 any other title, so that she learns proper respect.

I would have her taught the Bible, housewifery, writing and good works. Other learning a woman needs not . . . .
10 I pray God give her a wise and religious heart.

Elizabeth Josceline, *The Mother's Legacy to her Unborn Child (1622).*
Advice written when she was expecting her
15 *first baby, in case she died in childbirth.*

2 Good manners

Fathers . . . cause your children to use fair and gentle speech . . . with respect and politeness to their elders . . . .

Don't dress your children in rich 20 clothing . . . . Neither let your children go where they want, but know where they go . . . and when you hear them swear or curse, lie or fight, you shall sharply tell them off 25

Children . . . don't speak with your mouth full, nor scratch your head when you are eating, nor spit on the table.

Hugh Rhodes, *School of Good Manners (1570)* 30

3 An Elizabethan school. How does it compare with your own school?

4 A lady talks to her daughters

Daughters	I beseech you, Mother, pray to God to bless me, and give me your blessing, if it pleaseth you.
Lady	I pray the strong Almightie God to blesse you . . . . Now Fleurimonde, have you prayed to God today?
Fleurimonde	Yes forsooth, Mother.
Lady	Fleurimonde, showe me your worke: is this your Needle-worke? Me thinketh that it is somewhat wrong: I espie a fault in it, though the edge is reasonably well-made. Is this your lace-worke? See how she frowns! If I begin with you I will make you stop frowning: and you Charlotte, where is your worke? Are your tapestry cushens ended?
Charlotte	I have only one cushen to do, but I lack silk, I know not what is become of the canvas, all my gold and silver is finished . . . .
Lady	Ask the steward for some. At what hours do your Masters come?
Charlotte	Our dancing Master commeth about nine a clocke, our singing Master at tenne: he that teacheth us on the Lute at four a clocke in the after noone: and our French Master commeth between seven and eight a clocke in the morning.
Lady	It is then time to go study your lessons . . . . Now go in God's name – I goe to the Nurses' chamber, to see your brothers.

35

40

45

50

55

Peter Erondell, *The French Garden (c. 1605),
a book of plays written to teach pupils new words.*

❓ ❓ QUESTIONS ❓ ❓

1 Study sources 1–3. Make a list of all the rules and principles that the Tudors and Stuarts thought important in a child's upbringing.

2 Study source 4. Which of the rules on your list did the mother of Charlotte and Fleurimonde follow in the way she treated her daughters?

Overleaf: Children playing games, painted by Pieter Bruegel (1525–69).

Children's Games

Marriage

SHE was 14 years old, the daughter of the great lawyer, Sir Edward Coke. She was beautiful and strong-willed. Her name was Frances Coke.

5 HE was not the perfect bridegroom. He was 26. Every now and then he went mad and cut himself with broken glass. His name was John Villiers.

Frances's father wanted Villiers to 10 marry his daughter. Villiers was the brother of the powerful Duke of Buckingham, King James's favourite. Edward Coke hoped the marriage would make the king like him. He 15 offered Villiers a dowry (marriage payment) of £10,000 and £1,000 a year.

Frances's mother, Lady Hatton, did not want the marriage to take place. She 20 wanted Frances to marry the Earl of Oxford. To help things along, Lady Hatton forged love letters from the Earl. Then she forced Frances to promise to marry him.

25 Edward Coke forged a search warrant and went to get Frances. His men broke down the door, found her hiding in a cupboard and dragged her from the house. Lady Hatton went to court, got 30 a warrant, and took her daughter back at gunpoint.

Then King James became involved. He decided that Frances had to marry John Villiers. Frances was equally determined that she would not! 35

James tried to force her to do as he wanted. First, he sent the Earl of Oxford away, then he imprisoned Lady Hatton. Finally, Frances was 'tied to the bedposts and whipped'. 40

In the end, Frances agreed to marry John Villiers. She wrote to her mother:

I am a child and I don't understand what is good for me. Sir John Villiers is a gentleman and I do not dislike him. 45 Dear mother, believe me, there have been no violent means used to me in word or deed.

The wedding (on 29 September 1617) was magnificent, but – as might be 50 expected – the marriage was a disaster. After a time, John Villiers went completely mad. His land was given to his family. Then Frances became pregnant. The baby's father was a 55 young man at court called Sir Robert Howard. King James arrested Frances. She escaped to France and lived there with Robert Howard for the rest of her life, happy but poor. 60

Right: A husband beating his wife.

These sources will give you more information about married life:

1 My wife had a fit, just as she was sitting down after supper. At first she recovered, and spoke and kissed me, and complained only of a headache; but she fell down again in a quarter of an hour, and never spoke again.

   She was a lovely, beautiful, fair woman, a good Christian, funny and wise, yet the most sweet, affectionate and faithful wife in the world. She did well at anything she tried – housewifery, needlework, cookery. She was free from any pride, and full of good advice.

A letter written in 1649 by **Lord Shaftesbury** *after the death of his wife.*

2 A man met a friend he had not seen for a long time. His friend asked him how he was. He said he was very well, and had married since they last met.
   'That's good,' said his friend.
   'Not so good,' said he, 'for I have married a shrew.'
   'That's bad,' said his friend.
   'Not so bad,' said the man, 'for I got a dowry of £2,000 with her.'
   'That's good,' replied his friend . . . .
   'Not so good,' he said, 'for I bought a house, and it burned down.'
   'That's very bad,' his friend said.
   'Not so bad,' said he, 'for my wife was burned in it.'

From a seventeenth-century joke book.

3 Lord Cobham's family (sixteenth century). Lord and Lady Cobham had money and children, but did they love each other ?

My Lady Dresses

In Elizabethan times, the way that people had to dress was set down by law. Different classes were expected to dress according to their place in society.

Rich women took a great deal of care about the clothes they wore, as the play on page 31 shows. They also took a great deal of trouble with their make-up, although the poisonous lead powder they used to whiten their faces damaged their skin (and sometimes killed them). Many Elizabethan women, however, were slaves to fashion. When their skin was very damaged, they scrubbed it off, and started again on a new layer of skin!

An Elizabethan lady's beauty routine. This drawing is by a modern artist.

Eyes were treated with deadly nightshade to make them large and shining.

Hair was curled by wrapping it round sticks. It was oiled, scented – and full of lice.

Eyebrows were plucked and painted.

An evening wash in asses' milk and rose water was thought to whiten the face.

Lips and cheeks were painted with cochineal and egg-white. Alum made the flesh rough so the make-up would take hold.

Teeth were cleaned with the end of a stick, using honey, salt or brick dust.

The face, neck and chest were whitened with poisonous white lead powder, which damaged the skin.

If the face was badly marked, women stripped off the top layer of skin with almond paste or pumice stone.

Lady	Ho! Who is in the inner Chamber? Maidens, hear you not? Are you deaf?
Jolye	I am heere, Madam.
Lady	Will you keepe me heere all the day? Where be all my thinges? Goe fetch my clothes: bring my damask bodice with whale bones. This lace is too shorte, the tags are broken, I cannot lace myselfe with it, take it away. Give me my peticoate of Crimson velvet with silver fringe. I take colde; where be my stockens? Showe me my Carnation silk stockens; where laid you last night my garters? Take away these slippers, give me my velvet pantoufles. Jolye, come dresse my head. Set the Table further from the fire, it is too neere. I praye you Jolye, rubbe well my head, for it is very full of dandrufe. Where is my combe? Give me first my combing cloth, otherwise the haires will fall on my cloathes. O God! you combe too hard, you scratch me, you pull out my haires.
Jolye	Will it please you to rise up a little, Madame? For your hair is so long, that it trails on the ground.
Lady	Take the combe-brushes; take a quill to take away the filth from them. Take the key of my closet, and goe fetch the box where I put my Jewels that I use to wear on my head.
	Go too, give me some water to wash, where's my muske ball? Give me rather my paste of Almonds, for it scoureth better: where is my Scarlet cloth to wipe my face? Now set on my necklace of precious stones: call my Taylor to bring my open gowne of white satin layd on with buttons of Pearle. Shall I have no farthingale? You remember nothing, you have a rabbit's memory. Pass me my kirtle of green silk; go to it you head-braine, you doe nothing but playe the foole.
Jolye	What doth it please you to have, Madam, a ruff or a Rebato?
Lady	Let me see that ruff. Why is the supporter so dirty? I know not for what you are fit, you cannot so much as keep my cloathes cleane; take it away and give me my Rebato.

Peter Erondell, *The French Garden (c. 1605)*

5
10
15
20
25
30

damask: *white cloth, with decorations in white.*
bodice: *a kind of corset which made the waist look thinner and the bust look bigger.*
Crimson: *bright red.*
Carnation: *pink.*
pantoufles: *slippers.*
quill: *a sharpened feather.*
closet: *cupboard.*
muske ball: *a bag of perfume worn under the clothes.*
paste of Almonds: *a nut paste, used to scrub off the top layer of skin.*
Scarlet cloth: *she thought that using a red cloth would stop her getting the plague.*
farthingale: *a wooden frame to hold out the kirtle (the over-skirt).*
ruff: *a frilly collar round the neck.*
Rebato: *a high collar behind the head.*

35
40

Life on the Farm

What was life like for ordinary people in Tudor and Stuart times? Most people worked on the land, so perhaps the sources on these two pages can help us to find out.

During Tudor and Stuart times, many landowners in the south and east of England changed from growing crops to sheep farming. The landowners put up fences to enclose the land. This process was called enclosure. Fewer workers were needed for sheep-farming than for growing crops, so many farm workers lost their jobs.

In 1549, thousands of farm workers met at Mousehold Heath in Norfolk. They were led by Robert Ket, a local leather worker. They pulled down a few fences and captured Norwich. The rebellion was brutally put down, but attacks on enclosure fences were common for the next hundred years.

1 Study the picture below, particularly the things you can see going on in the background. Discuss the impression it gives of farm workers' lives. For instance, what are they wearing? What different jobs are being done? What were the most important buildings in the village? What sort of houses did ordinary people live in? What was their life like?

2 A ploughman's day

The ploughman shall rise before 4 o'clock in the morning, and after giving
thanks to God for his rest, he shall go into the stable, and first he shall feed his
cattle, then clean the barn, rub down the cattle and clean their skins from all dirt . . . .

5 And while the cattle are eating their food, he shall make ready his collars, harness and
plough-gears, seeing that everything is fit and in its proper place, and to this work I will
allow him two hours; that is from four o'clock till six.

Then he shall come in to breakfast, and to that I allow him half an hour, and then
another half hour to the yoking and gearing of his cattle, so that at seven he may set
forth on his work; and then he shall plough from 7 o'clock in the morning till 2 in the
10 afternoon.

Then he shall unyoke and bring home his cattle, and having rubbed them and cleaned
them, he shall feed them. Then shall the servants go in for their dinner, for which I allow
half an hour.

It will then be towards 4 o'clock; at which time he shall go to the cattle again and,
15 rubbing them down and cleaning their stalls, will give them more food; which done, he
shall go into the barns [and work there] . . . .

By this time it will draw past 6 o'clock; at which time he shall come in to supper, and
after supper he shall sit by the fireside, mend shoes for himself and the family, or prepare
thread for spinning, or pick and crush apples for cider, or else grind malt for making beer,
20 pick rushes for candles, or do some household work until it be fully 8 o'clock.

Then he shall take his lantern and candle, and go to see his cattle, and having cleaned
their stalls, he shall put down straw for them, see that they are safely tied, and then give
them food for the night.

Then, giving God thanks for all the day's blessings, let him and the whole household go
25 to their rest till the next morning.

Gervase Markham, *Farewell to Husbandry (1653).*
Markham was a poet and writer of books on country life.

? ? ? QUESTIONS ? ? ?

1 How does source 2 give a different impression from that given by source 1?
2 Suggest five reasons why source 2 cannot be accepted as a description of the 'normal day' of a person living in Tudor and Stuart times.
3 Which source, do you think, is likely to give the better picture of what a farm worker's life was *really* like? Explain your answer.

TUDOR RELIGION

In the reign of Henry VIII, almost everybody in England was a Roman Catholic Christian. But, mixed into the Christian Catholic faith, there were thousands of superstitions.

The superstitions on these pages will give you some idea of what most people believed in Tudor times.

Ghosts were said to come out between midnight and dawn. It was thought that they might have a message to give you – a ghost could tell you who was going to die that year. But they ran away when they heard a cock crow.

If you tripped over the doorstep, you would find trouble when you went into the house.

If you said five Paternosters (the Lord's Prayer) and five Ave Marias (a prayer to the Virgin Mary) every day, you would have a good life, and die peacefully.

If you heard magpies chattering, guests would visit your house.

Most villages had a 'cunning man' or a 'wise woman', who people believed had special powers. Most of them used charms and magic spells. People would go to them for advice.

It was an omen of bad luck if you heard an owl hoot, or if a hare ran in front of you.

Carrying bay leaves would protect you from danger in a thunderstorm.

Many people wore a charm made out of wax from the church candles. It had a picture of a lamb on it, and was called the *agnus dei* ('the Lamb of God', one of the names of Jesus Christ). It was said to protect you against thunder, lightning, fire, drowning or death in childbirth.

Many people believed in goblins. One was called Puck (or Robin Goodfellow). If the dairy-maid left out a bowl of cream for him, he would help with household tasks. If he was forgotten, he might wash the children with beer, knock over buckets, or steal the milk.

You could tell the price of corn by seeing which way the seeds jumped when you put them on a hot hearth.

Sprinkling holy water from the church could drive away evil spirits, protect the family against the plague and cure diseases. It could also make your food more nutritious.

People stole the bread they were given at the service of the Mass. It was said to cure blindness and fevers. It would kill caterpillars if you crushed it and put it on your vegetables. It could put out fires, make your fields more fertile, help the bees make more honey and cure swine fever.

If you heard a raven croak, someone close to you would get ill with the plague.

People who could read often consulted almanacs (books of astrology) when they had to make a decision.

It was bad luck to plough, go on a journey, or cut your nails on a Friday.

The sign of the cross would frighten away evil spirits and protect you from danger. It was especially important to make the sign of the cross when you shut a window, left the cattle or went out of the house.

If you got up early in the morning, you might see fairies dancing in a fairy ring. But fairies stole babies. One way to stop them was to hang a knife over the baby's cradle.

Certain days were 'dismal days', when it was bad luck to begin a new task, get married, or go to the doctor's. The last Monday in December (Judas Iscariot's birthday) was especially unlucky.

If your child could not sleep, putting a Bible on the bed would give a good night's rest.

It was bad luck to:
- get out of bed on the 'wrong' side,
- have 13 people eating round a table,
- whistle after dark,
- kill a swallow, or
- spill salt.

People believed in witches. A witch could make it rain. Or she could hurt you. For instance, if a witch said the Lord's Prayer backwards and dropped holy candle wax onto a man's footprints, she could make his feet rot off.

It was good luck if:
- you found a four-leaved clover, or
- someone spilt a drink over you.

Changes in the Church

The two pictures on this page show what an English church might have looked like, first in 1533 (right), then in 1570 (below).

List all the differences you can see.

1 Rood screen*.
2 Service book in Latin.
3 Priest.
4 Stone altar, against the east wall of the church.
5 Candles.
6 Statue of the Virgin Mary.
7 Stained-glass windows.
8 Nave*.
9 Colourful paintings on the walls.
10 Altar rail.

* The rood screen was a screen with a cross (a 'rood') on it, separating the altar from the nave, where the ordinary people sat.

1 Pulpit for preaching.
2 Book of Common Prayer in English.
3 Minister.
4 Plain Communion table, pulled away from the east wall of the church.
5 Royal coat of arms.
6 Bible in English.
7 Plain glass windows.
8 Wall tablets on which the Ten Commandments and the Lord's Prayer are written.
9 Plain, whitewashed walls.

Catholics and Protestants

In the years between 1533 and 1570, England rejected the Roman Catholic religion and adopted a new kind of Christianity. This new religion had started in Germany. Its leader was a monk called Martin Luther.

In Rome, the popes were building huge churches and decorating them with beautiful works of art. To raise enough money, they sold indulgences (a 'guarantee' of your place in heaven). In 1517, Luther protested about this, and about many other things that he said were wrong with the Church. For this reason, he and his supporters were called 'Protestants'. Many areas of Germany threw out the Roman Catholic Church. They wanted to reform the Church; this is why this period is sometimes called 'the Reformation'.

The table below shows how Protestantism was different from Catholicism:

Roman Catholics	Protestants
The Pope is Head of the Church.	The local ruler should control the Church.
The local Church should be ruled by bishops.	The Church should be run by elders, elected by the people.
The priest brings Christ to the people, in the service of the Mass.	A minister must preach to the people, to tell them what the Bible says.
At the service of the Mass, the bread and wine turn into the body and blood of Jesus (transubstantiation).	The Communion service is just a service to remember Jesus's death. The bread wine stay as bread and wine.
There should be statues of the saints and the Virgin Mary in church. Saints and the Virgin Mary can take a person's prayers to God.	Statues of the saints and the Virgin Mary are as bad as idols. Only Jesus can take a person's prayers to God.
Services and the Bible should be in Latin.	Services and the Bible should be in English, so people can understand them.
A person is saved by going to church and doing good works.	A person is saved by one thing only – a personal faith in Jesus Christ.
Priests should wear bright robes, and churches should have colourful paintings and beautiful music, to show how great God is.	Ministers' clothes and churches should be plain, so people can concentrate on God. There should not be any music in the services.
Priests must not marry.	Ministers can marry.

Religious Changes

The twenty-five years after 1533 saw great changes in religion in England.

Henry VIII

Henry VIII had broken away from the Pope, so he was no longer a Roman

5 Catholic – but he was fiercely Catholic. In 1539, Henry passed the Six Articles. Priests who married, and anyone who did not believe in transubstantiation (see page 37), would be burned to death.

10 Ordinary people were forbidden to read the Bible. About five hundred Protestants were arrested, and some were burned to death (including a woman called Anne Askew, who was so cruelly tortured that

15 she had to be carried to the stake).

This painting from 1548 celebrates Edward VI's Reformation of the Church. On the left, Henry VIII gives Edward his blessing. On the right are the Duke of Somerset and the royal Council. Beneath

20 Edward's feet, the Pope and monks are crushed by the Bible. Through the window reformers can be seen smashing statues of the saints and the Virgin Mary.

Edward VI

When Henry died in 1547, his son Edward was only nine years old. He

25 was too young to rule on his own, so a regent ruled the country for him. Edward's first regent was his uncle, Edward Seymour, the Duke of Somerset, who was a Protestant.

30 Under Somerset, there was a religious revolution in England. The Latin Mass was abolished and a new prayer book was published – in the English language. Statues of the saints were

35 smashed, and pictures on church walls were whitewashed. Stone altars were thrown out, and replaced by wooden Communion tables. Protestant missionaries were sent out to different

40 parts of England, with Bibles, to teach people the new ways.

Many people hated the new services.
In 1549 the people of Devon and
45 Cornwall rose in rebellion against the
new prayer book saying that 'it is but
like a Christmas game'. The rebels
were defeated, and the priests who had
led it were hanged from their own
50 steeples.

The Duke of Somerset fell from
power, but his successor, the Duke of
Northumberland, was even more
fiercely Protestant. A new, stricter
55 prayer book was published. Catholic
bishops were sent to the Tower.

Mary

And then everything changed.
Edward died in 1553, and Mary
(Henry's elder daughter) became queen.
60 She was a Catholic, and wanted to
make England a Roman Catholic
country once again.

The Catholic bishops came out of the
Tower; Protestant ministers went in.
65 Mary brought back the Latin church
services and Bibles. She was advised by
Reginald Pole, an English Cardinal
who came to England from Rome.
In 1554 Queen and Parliament knelt
70 before him and begged to be reunited
with Rome. In the same year, Mary
married the son of the King of Spain,
Prince Philip. Spain was a Catholic
country.

Mary and Philip. Their marriage caused a   75
rebellion in Kent, led by Thomas Wyatt. Mary
defeated the rebels. Wyatt and about ninety of
his followers were tortured and executed. Philip
never loved Mary, and spent most of his time in
Spain. Mary was very unhappy.   80

Mary offered the Protestants a choice:
'Turn or Burn'. About three hundred
Protestants chose to be burned. But
times had changed in England. Many
of Mary's victims, ordinary people, died   85
like heroes. The burnings did not turn
people back to Rome, they made
people hate Roman Catholicism. Mary
became more and more unpopular.
People started to call her 'Bloody   90
Mary'. When she died in 1558, people
rejoiced.

Elizabeth I
Elizabeth, Henry's younger daughter,
became queen in 1558. There had been
twenty-five years of swings to and fro   95
between Catholicism and Protestantism.

In France, religious differences led to a
civil war which almost destroyed the
country. Was the same going to
happen in England?   100

39

Burned at the Stake!

Queen Mary believed that heretics – people who did not agree with her Catholic religion – had to be burned. The fire would be a punishment, but it would also burn away their sin.

Two of the Protestants who were burned were Hugh Latimer and Nicholas Ridley. Latimer was a preacher who criticised rich people, as well as the Catholic religion. Ridley was the Bishop of London.

John Foxe (1516-87) was a Protestant writer. His *Book of Martyrs* (1563) described Mary's persecution of the Protestants in great detail. It is a very biased source – it strongly favours the Protestants and is very critical of Mary.

A Protestant woodcut from the sixteenth century showing the death of Latimer and Ridley.

The death of Latimer and Ridley

Then the smith took a chain of iron, and brought the same about both
Dr. Ridley's and Master Latimer's middles. Then Dr. Ridley's brother-in-law did
bring him gunpowder in a bag, and would have tied the same about his neck.
Master Ridley asked what it was. His brother said, 'Gunpowder.' 'Then,' said he, 'I take it

5 to be sent of God; therefore I will use it – and have you any,' said he, 'for my brother;'
so his brother-in-law went and carried of the same unto Master Latimer . . . .

Then they brought a faggot, kindled with fire, and laid the same down at Dr. Ridley's
feet. To him Master Latimer spoke in this manner: 'Be of good comfort, Master Ridley,
and play the man. We shall this day light such a candle in England, by God's grace,

10 as I trust shall never be put out.'

And so the fire being given to them, when Dr. Ridley saw the fire flaming up towards
him he cried, 'Into Your hand, O Lord, I give my spirit;' Master Latimer crying as earnestly
on the other side, 'O Father of heaven, receive my soul!'

Master Latimer received the flame as it were embracing it. After he had stroked his

15 face with his hands and, as it were, bathed them a little in the fire, he soon died (so it
appeareth) with very little pain or none . . . .

But Master Ridley, by reason of the evil making of the fire unto him, because the
wooden faggots were laid about the gorse, and over-high built, the fire burned first
beneath, being kept down by the wood; which, when he felt, he desired them for Christ's

20 sake to let the fire come unto him. Which, when his brother-in-law heard, intending to rid
him out of his pain, as one in sorrow not well-advised in what he did, heaped more
faggots upon him, so that he clean covered him, which made the fire more vehement
beneath, that it burned clean all his lower parts, before it once touched the upper.
Therefore he leapt up and down under the faggots, and often desired them to let the fire

25 come unto him, saying, 'I cannot burn.' Which indeed appeared true; for, after his legs
were consumed, he showed one side to us clean, shirt and all untouched with flame.

Yet in all his torment he forgot not to call upon God still, having in his mouth, 'Lord
have mercy upon me,' intermingling his cry, 'Let the fire come to me, I cannot burn.' In
which pain he laboured until one of the standers-by with a bill-hook pulled off the faggots

30 above, and where he saw the fire flame up, he pulled himself unto that side.
And when the flame touched the gunpowder, he was seen to stir no more.

John Foxe, *Book of Martyrs (1563)*

gunpowder: *a small bag of gunpowder was tied round the victims' necks, to kill them quickly.*
faggot: *bundle of wood.*
35 **vehement**: *fierce.*

? ? ? QUESTION ? ? ?

Do you think that burning people at the stake was a good way to stop Protestantism? Explain your answer.

Elizabeth's Middle Way

In 1571, Elizabeth published *The Thirty-nine Articles* of the Church of England (even today, priests have 39 buttons down the front of their cassocks).

Elizabeth tried to follow a Middle Way in religion, which both Catholics and Protestants could accept:

Roman Catholics	Elizabeth's Middle Way	Protestants
The Pope is Head of the Church.	The Queen is Supreme Governor of the Church in England.	The local ruler should control the Church.
The local Church should be ruled by bishops.	There is nothing wrong with bishops, but they must be under the control of the Queen.	The Church should be run by elders, elected by the people.
The priest brings Christ to the people, in the service of the Mass.	People must have their own faith, but only properly ordained priests can preach in church.	A minister must preach to the people, to tell them what the Bible says.
At the service of the Mass, the bread and wine turn into the body and blood of Jesus (transubstantiation).	The bread and wine do not change – they stay as bread and wine. But Christ is 'really present' in the bread and wine, in a spiritual way.	The Communion service is just a service to remember Jesus's death. The bread and wine stay as bread and wine.
There should be statues of the saints and the Virgin Mary in church. Saints and the Virgin Mary can take a person's prayers to God.	A person should not pray to saints. There should be no statues in churches. But the Church can celebrate saints' days.	Statues of the saints and the Virgin Mary are as bad as idols. Only Jesus can take a person's prayers to God.
Services and the Bible should be in Latin.	Services and the Bible should be in English.	Services and the Bible should be in English, so people can understand them.
A person is saved by going to church and by doing good works.	A person is saved by faith, but a person with faith will do good works, because it pleases God.	A person is saved by one thing only – a personal faith in Jesus Christ.
Priests should wear bright robes, and churches should have colourful paintings and beautiful music, to show how great God is.	Churches must be kept clean and in good repair. They can be decorated. There can be music. Priests should wear special robes.	Ministers' clothes and churches should be plain, so people can concentrate on God. There should not be any music in the services.
Priests must not marry.	Priests can marry (but Elizabeth did not really approve of married priests).	Ministers can marry.

Elizabeth's problems

Elizabeth wanted a Middle Way in religion, but people who did not follow it were punished.

Some extreme Protestants (called Puritans) wanted to get rid of bishops and special robes for priests. Elizabeth put them in prison. At the same time, Catholics who did not go to church (recusants) were fined.

Catholics were Elizabeth's biggest problem. Her enemies tried to get them to rebel against her. Elizabeth could never be sure that the English Catholics were loyal.

Many Catholics plotted against the queen. Those who were caught were tortured and executed. So were the 130 Catholic priests who were captured during her reign.

When Edmund Campion was arrested for treason in 1581, he was starved and left to the rats. Iron spikes were pushed under his fingernails and toenails. He was hanged, then cut down while he was still alive and quartered. Through all this he was cheerful and never denied his Catholic faith. Was he a hero – or a traitor?

Catholic priests were hunted down by Elizabeth's soldiers. They tried to avoid capture by disguising themselves, and by hiding in priest holes in the large houses belonging to rich Catholics.

When they were caught, they were tortured and executed. The priest in this picture is being dragged off to be executed.

43

PHILIP II OF SPAIN

King Philip's Problems

Philip II of Spain ruled the greatest empire the world had ever known.

Philip was a devout Catholic. He believed that it was his duty to rule fairly and to care for his subjects. He was hard-working and patient.

Spanish troops had destroyed the Aztec and Inca empires in the New World. Philip's cousin, Rudolph, was ruler of Austria-Hungary and Emperor of Germany. In addition, the Pope was a friend of Spain.

When Philip conquered Portugal in 1580, his empire included almost all of the explored world.

Spain's empire in 1580
1 Spain.
2 Portugal.
3 The Netherlands.
4 Franche Comté (in Germany).
5 Milan and Naples in Italy.
6 Sicily and Sardinia.
7 Florida in North America.
8 Mexico.
9 Cuba, Hispaniola and many islands in the West Indies.
10 Venezuela, Peru, Chile and Brazil in South America.
11 Angola and Mozambique in Africa and the island of Madagascar.
12 Colonies in India and Ceylon.
13 Oman in Arabia.
14 The Philippines and other islands in Indonesia.

Philip ruled his vast empire from the palace that he built at Escorial, near Madrid.

SCENOGRAPHIA FABRICÆ S. LAVRENTII IN ESCVR

King Philip faced many problems. These are some of them:

1 In 1572, Protestants in the Netherlands rebelled against Spain. Elizabeth I of England sent troops and money to the Dutch rebels.

16 In 1587, Elizabeth I of England executed Mary, Queen of Scots, for plotting to take the throne of England. Mary was a Catholic who had made Philip her heir.

2 The rulers of the Ottoman (Turkish) Empire were enemies of Spain. In 1580, England signed a trade treaty with Turkey.

15 In 1580, Philip invaded Portugal. Don Antonio, his Portuguese rival, escaped to England. Elizabeth I promised to help him attack Philip.

3 France was an enemy of Spain. In 1581 the Duke of Anjou led a French army to help the Dutch, and signed a marriage treaty with Elizabeth I of England.

14 In 1587, the English privateer Sir Francis Drake attacked the port of Cadiz in Spain.

4 England was an enemy of Spain. In 1581, England had laws forbidding the Catholic religion.

13 In 1587, the English set up a colony in North America, called Virginia after Elizabeth I (the Virgin Queen).

5 It was difficult to rule the huge empire. It took Philip months to reply to letters.

12 Because it cost Philip so much to keep the Spanish army in the Netherlands, he often had money troubles.

6 English 'privateers' (pirates such as Sir Francis Drake) attacked Spanish treasure ships.

11 In Spain there were a few Protestants. Philip had them burned at the stake.

7 Dutch 'sea beggars' (pirates) attacked Spanish ships. Elizabeth I allowed them to use English ports.

10 In 1569, the Spanish Moriscos – Muslims who had become Christians – rebelled. Philip expelled them from Spain.

8 English and Dutch traders took slaves to Spain's colonies in America. Philip had ordered that only Spanish ships could trade with the New World.

9 In 1568, three Spanish treasure ships sheltered from a storm in Southampton, England. Elizabeth I confiscated them.

The Armada

Philip decided to invade England. He planned to gather an army in the Netherlands. Then a huge armada (fleet) of ships would take the army across to England. In February 1588, Philip's commander in the Netherlands reported that an army of thirty thousand men was ready.

In May 1588, an 'Invincible Armada' of 130 ships set sail from Lisbon in Portugal.

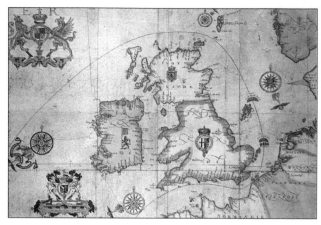

The route of the Armada.

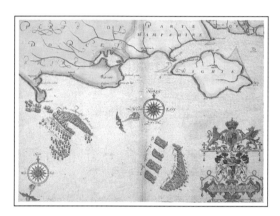

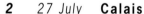

1 19 July The English Channel
Left: The Armada reached the English Channel. It took up a defensive crescent (half-moon) formation. The English fleet chased it. There was a series of battles, but only three Spanish ships were lost.

The map shows two events. On the left, a battle is in progress. On the right, four English fleets are chasing the Spanish ships.

2 27 July Calais
Below: The Spanish fleet anchored near Calais, but Philip's troops were not ready. Next day, the English sent fireships into the Spanish fleet. The Spanish ships cut their anchors and fled out to sea. In the panic, one ship crashed into another and ran aground.

3   29 July   Battle of Gravelines

Above: The Spanish were no longer in formation. They sailed into the North Sea. The English ships attacked them for six days. The Spanish sailors fought bravely. Four Spanish ships were lost, but many others were badly damaged.

English warships were longer and narrower than the Spanish galleons. They could turn more quickly than the Spanish ships, especially in bad weather. Also, the gun-ports were larger than on Spanish ships, so the gunners could see where they were firing.

4   7 August   The Great Gale

Right: The Spanish ships tried to make their way home round the north of Scotland. They had little food or ammunition left; many sailors died of starvation. Storms separated the Spanish fleet. It is thought that 35 Spanish ships were lost.

5   Late August   Ireland

Left: At least 20 ships were wrecked on the coast of Ireland. Spanish sailors who managed to get ashore were put to death by the English soldiers in Ireland. During September, 67 damaged ships limped back to Spain. The invasion had failed.

All on Board!

What was life like on one of the ships in the Armada? Nobody knows.
We do, however, have a description by a Spaniard, Eugenio de Salazar,
who sailed across the Atlantic in 1573. The *Nuestra Señora* ('Our Lady')
was a small ship, about twenty years old, with a crew of thirty sailors.
Eugenio wrote to a friend:

To Miranda de Ron:

I write to tell you about my sufferings at sea; though I must admit that they included (thank God)
no pirates or shipwrecks.

The movement of the sea upset our stomachs so horribly that we all turned white as ghosts and
began to bring up our very souls; we vomited, we gagged, we shot out of our mouths everything which
5   had gone in during the last two days.

A ship is a long narrow city, sharp and pointed at one end, wider at the other; it has its streets,
open spaces and dwellings; it is encircled by its walls – that is to say, its planking. It has one or two
fountains, called pumps, the water from which is unfit for tongue to taste, or nostrils to smell. The
dwellings are so closed-in, dark and evil-smelling that they seem more like burial holes, or the caves
10   of Hell. There is such a complicated network of ropes and rigging that the men inside it are like hens
being carried to market.

For game in the neighbourhood there are fine flights of cockroaches, and very good rat-hunting,
rats so fierce that when they are cornered they turn on the hunters like wild boars. There are lice so
enormous that sometimes they are seasick and vomit out bits of sailor.

15   The sailors are all rogues. But I have never seen a gang of rogues obey more promptly; for when the
captain shouts they come tumbling in a moment, like conjured demons. Some will be up on the main
masts; some riding on the yards, holding on to the sails; some on deck, hauling and gathering; some
climbing and swinging about in the rigging like monkeys in the trees.

And when they hoist the sails – to hear the sailors singing as they work! for they hoist to the
20   time of their song. The leader calls out:

Bu iza - o dio - ayuta noi – o que somo - servi soy - o voleamo.

All the others reply in chorus: 'Oh – Oh', and haul away to hoist the sail.

Then I would see the ship's boys emerge from the half-deck with a bundle of cloths. They spread
these out and on them put little mounds of broken biscuit. They would then place on this 'table' a
25   few beefbones, with bits of sinew clinging to them. When the meal is laid out, one of the boys sings
out: 'All hands to dinner! If you don't come, you won't eat!' In a twinkling, out come pouring all the
ship's company saying 'Amen' who, without pausing, whip out their knives and daggers and fall upon
those poor bones. It is like an ant heap. Men and women, young and old, clean and dirty, are all mixed
up together. The people around you will belch or vomit, or break wind, or empty their bowels while you
30   are having your breakfast.

If you want to empty your bowels, you have to hang out over the sea like a cat-burglar clinging to a
wall. Your only hope is to wait until you are desperate.

The worst longing is for something to drink; you are in the middle of the sea, surrounded by water,
but they dole it out in thimbles, and all the time you are dying of thirst from eating dried beef and
35   food pickled in salt.

Doña Catalina and the children send their respects and best wishes.

Eugenio de Salazar

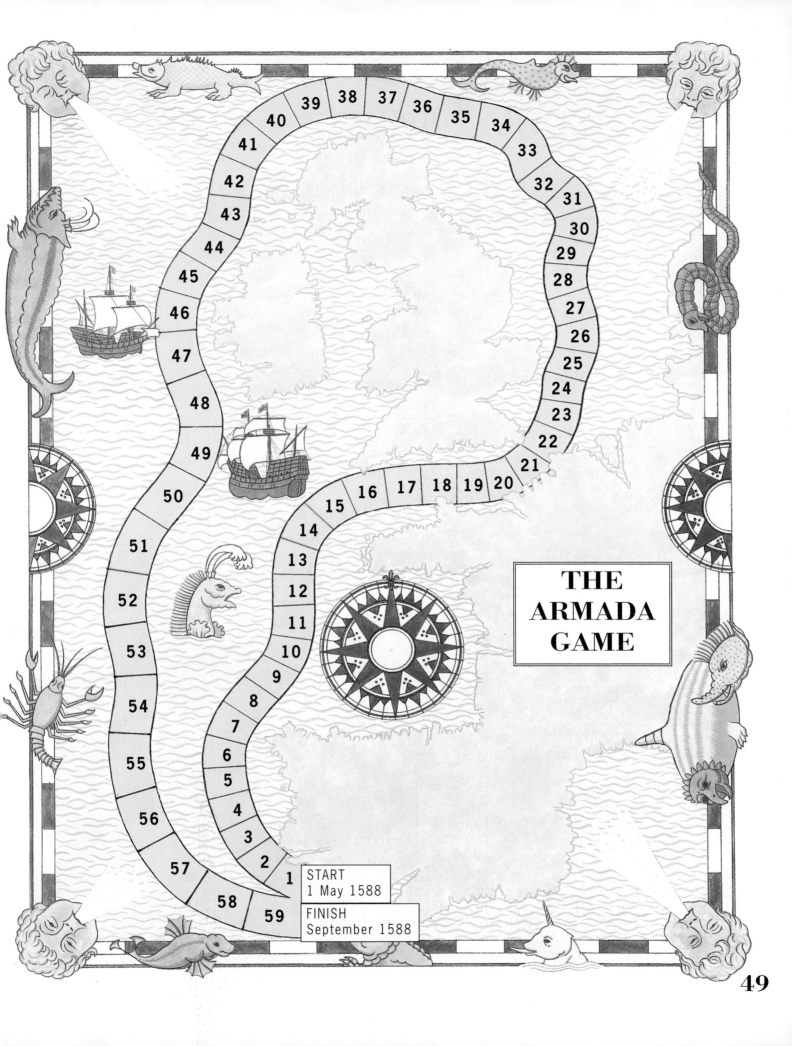

THE
ARMADA
GAME

START
1 May 1588

FINISH
September 1588

49

A KINGDOM DIVIDED

The Causes of the Civil War

The main issues of the sixteenth century in England had been the power of the king, and arguments about religion.

In the seventeenth century, these issues caused a civil war.

William Laud

Many MPs were Puritans (extreme
5 Protestants). They wanted the country to
be more Protestant.

But after the Gunpowder Plot (1605),
people were afraid that Catholics were
becoming powerful again. In 1625, King
10 Charles I married Henrietta Maria, a
Roman Catholic from France.

In 1633, William Laud became
Archbishop of
Canterbury. Laud did
15 not make church services
more Protestant. Instead,
he told ministers to put
the Communion table
back at the east end of
20 the church, and to
decorate it with cloths,
candles and a cross.
People were told to bow
at the name of Jesus.

25 Laud's religious rules
made many people
angry. To the Puritans,
they were no better than
superstition and idol-
30 worship.

A church in the time of Archbishop Laud. Compare this picture with the drawings on page 36.

Were Laud's changes really a return to the Catholic religion? 35

William Noy

For almost a century, prices had been rising steadily.

The rise in prices caused great hardship. Poor people were angry
40 about inflation, and they blamed the king.

At the same time, landowners (including the king) who collected rents, were also affected. Their
45 incomes fell behind the cost of living. As a result, Charles was always short of money.

Charles did not ask Parliament to give him more money. Instead, he
50 asked a clever lawyer called William Noy to discover old, forgotten laws and taxes. People were angry about the tricks Charles used to raise money.

55 The rise in prices made many merchants and businessmen very wealthy.

Four annoying taxes

1 Knighthoods
A law of 1278 said that anyone who earned more than £40 a year had to become a knight. In the Middle Ages, £40 was a huge sum 60 of money. In the seventeenth century, however, many ordinary people earned more than £40 a year and so were forced to pay money to become a knight. 65

2 Forest laws
In the Middle Ages, it was against the law to take land that was part of a royal forest. Charles fined anyone who had taken royal land.

3 Monopolies
Charles sold people the right to be 70 the only trader in a wide range of goods – for example, salt, soap, currants and mousetraps. The traders then raised prices and made huge profits. 75

4 Ship money
In the Middle Ages, people who lived in seaports had paid a tax to build ships for the king's navy in times of war. Charles not only revived this old tax, but also made 80 *all* towns pay it – even if they were miles inland and the country was at peace! In 1637 the MP John Hampden refused to pay ship money. 85

51

Divine Right

Charles did not use the ordinary courts, and trial by jury, to enforce his out-of-date laws. He used his private Court of the Star Chamber, where there was no
90 jury, and where the judges were the king's own ministers.

Charles also used the Court of the Star Chamber to punish Puritans. In 1637 a Puritan called William Prynne was fined
95 £5,000 and imprisoned for life. His ears were cut off and his cheeks were branded.

Many people were angry about the Court of the Star Chamber. They said
100 that the king should not have his own court, and that he should follow the law of the land.

Charles believed that his power came directly from God. This is called the
105 Divine Right of Kings. Charles said that it put him above the ordinary laws.

This cartoon shows Laud eating William Prynne's ears, while Prynne holds a bandage to his head. Laud did not really eat Prynne's ears. The
110 cartoon shows us that people were very angry about the way Charles had treated Prynne.

War

King James had signed a peace treaty with Spain in 1604, and in 1625 Charles married Henrietta Maria of France. Both France and Spain were Roman Catholic 115 countries. Many Puritans were angry because they wanted Charles to fight 'holy wars' against Catholic countries.

When Charles finally went to war, his foreign policy was a disaster! Attacks on 120 Spain (1625) and France (1627-28) were complete failures – and England ended up at war with both Spain and France. Now people were angry because Charles could not win the wars he had started. 125

The Eleven Years' Tyranny

Parliament complained to the king. In 1628, MPs presented Charles with the Petition of Right. It said that the king had no right to raise taxes without Parliament's consent, or to imprison 130 people without a fair trial.

Instead of listening, Charles sent Parliament away. Between 1629 and 1640 he ruled by himself without a parliament. People were angry and called 135 this time 'the Eleven Years' Tyranny'.

Royal favourites

The king gave power and money to his advisers – men such as George Villiers, the Duke of Buckingham. The way
140 Charles treated his royal favourites made many people angry.

One of Charles's chief advisers was Thomas Wentworth, the Earl of Strafford. As Lord Deputy of Ireland,
145 Strafford had used the army to enforce Charles's laws. People were alarmed when Charles recalled him to England in 1639. They were afraid that Strafford was going to use the same methods in
150 England as he had done in Ireland.

The Bishops' Wars

In 1637, Laud tried to make the people of Scotland obey his Church of England rules. The result was the Bishops' Wars. The Scots invaded the north of England.
155 The war against Scotland was expensive. In 1640 the king was forced to bring back Parliament to ask them to give him money for the war.

The Grand Remonstrance

The MPs were led by a lawyer called John Pym. They refused to grant any money until the king promised to listen to their complaints.

In November 1641, Parliament 165 presented a Grand Remonstrance (big protest) against Charles's taxes, courts and religious rules. The Star Chamber was abolished. In addition, Parliament tried to reduce the power of bishops, to 170 choose the king's ministers and to control the army. The Earl of Strafford and William Laud were found guilty of treason and executed.

The last straw

The final straw came on 4 January 175 1642. Charles tried to arrest John Pym, John Hampden and three other MPs: Hazelrigg, Holles and Strode. They escaped, but people were very angry that Charles had tried to arrest the 180 five MPs.

Charles left London. In August, he declared war on Parliament.

The Scots rebelled when Laud tried to force them
160 to use the English prayer book.

QUESTIONS

1 When you have read pages 50–53, make a list of 12 different things which made English people angry or afraid.
2 Divide your list into three categories, saying whether each thing was a political, economic or religious issue.

A Time to Decide

People had to choose between the 'Cavaliers' on the king's side, and the 'Roundheads' who supported Parliament. Should they take up arms (fight) for the king or for Parliament?

The nation was divided. Friends and family often disagreed with each other. It was time to decide.

A Royalist (Cavalier) might:

- believe in the Divine Right of Kings;
- agree that Charles had the right to take taxes such as ship money and grant monopolies when he wanted;
- support the bishops, and agree with Archbishop Laud's reforms in the Church of England;
- think that people ought to obey the king, and that it was wrong to go to war against him.

These pictures show a Cavalier (above) and a Roundhead (right) as we imagine them today.

In real life, things were not so clear cut. Few people dressed like this, and people often found it difficult to decide which side to support.

A seventeenth-century picture of a shepherd.

Most poor people fought for whichever side their landlord supported. Some people did not know or care about the issues. In 1644, when an army patrol near Marston Moor told a shepherd that the king and Parliament were at war, he said: 'Whaat! Has them two fallen out then?'

A Parliamentarian (Roundhead) might:

- believe that Parliament should make the laws and govern the nation;
- believe in the principle of no taxation without Parliament's agreement;
- hate the bishops and want Puritan reforms to make the Church of England more Protestant;
- have no personal loyalty to the king, and believe that there was no need to obey the king if he was wrong.

The Civil War

1642

The Civil War started on 22 August 1642, when Charles I raised his standard in Nottingham. Most of Parliament's support came from the south and the
5 east of the country. The king held the north, Wales and the West Country.

The first big battle of the war was fought on 23 October 1642, at Edgehill in Warwickshire. The royal cavalry, led
10 by the king's nephew, Prince Rupert, defeated Parliament's cavalry, but then turned away to chase the enemy. The result was a confused draw.

The battle horrified a Puritan
15 landowner and MP from East Anglia called Oliver Cromwell. He saw how good the king's cavalry was:

Our troops are most of them old serving men, and their troops are
20 gentlemen's sons and persons of quality. Do you think our poor fellows will ever be able to defeat gentlemen that have courage and determination?

Cromwell went back to East Anglia to
25 train an army of men 'who had the fear of God before them'.

Charles advanced towards London, but thousands of citizens turned out to stop him. They built earth mounds and put
30 snipers in every cottage, shed and hedge. On 12 November 1642, at Turnham Green, Charles was forced to turn back.

1643

In 1643, the king planned a campaign which he hoped would win the war. Three Royalist armies advanced on 35 London at the same time – one from the North, one from Cornwall, and a third from the king's headquarters at Oxford.

The plan failed. The southern army 40 was held up at Bristol, and the northern army was held up at Hull. Finally, the king failed to defeat Parliament's army at Newbury (20 September 1643) because he ran out of ammunition. 45

A map of the Civil War.

KEY

Areas supporting the king in 1642.

Areas supporting Parliament in 1642.

Three-pronged attack of 1643.

1644

Slowly, Parliament began to win.

The navy supported Parliament, so Parliament captured all the ports. This
50 stopped Charles getting help from abroad. Parliament raised large sums of money – it put a new tax on food. Charles began to run out of money. Also, on 23 November 1643, Parliament
55 had joined forces with the Scots, who sent an army of twenty thousand men to fight the king.

Most importantly of all, Cromwell's new soldiers were now ready for battle.
60 The 'Ironsides' were well trained and well disciplined. They spent their spare time praying and talking about politics. On 2 July 1644, at Marston Moor near York, they made a surprise attack when
65 the Royalists were having their evening meal. About three thousand Royalist soldiers were killed.

1645

On 3 April 1645, Parliament re-organised its army along the lines
70 of Cromwell's Ironsides. They called it the New Model Army.

On 14 June 1645, the New Model Army destroyed the king's forces at
90 Naseby in Northamptonshire. The king fled. Many of his soldiers were killed or captured. He lost all his guns, his supplies and his private papers.

1646–48

The king had lost. On 5 May 1646, he
95 surrendered to the Scots at Newark. Both Parliament and the New Model Army tried to come to an agreement with the king.

Charles schemed and lied. On
100 26 December 1647 he made a treaty with the Scots, who invaded England. This was the start of the Second Civil War (1 May 1648).

The Second Civil War ended on
105 20 August 1648, when Cromwell defeated the Scots at Preston in Lancashire. Cromwell and the soldiers were furious with the king. They promised to 'call Charles Stuart, that
110 man of blood, to account'.

Right: Prince Rupert hiding in a beanfield after the battle of Marston Moor.
75   Rupert had a large white dog called Boy; many Parliamentary soldiers thought Boy was an evil spirit which
80 helped Rupert win battles.

What have the soldiers found?

What colour is Boy in
85 the picture? Why?

Which side did the artist support?

york

Civil Warfare

Army commanders in the Civil War still fought 'pitched' battles, which meant that the time and the place were arranged beforehand. The two sides organised their forces in battle lines, facing each other.

They put the infantry (foot soldiers – pikemen and musketeers) in the centre of the line. The cavalry (soldiers on horseback) were put on the flanks (sides) of the army. The armies charged at each other.

But whether the battle was won or lost depended on the cavalry.

For the king, Prince Rupert was a brave cavalry commander. He and his men made a wild charge which almost always drove his opponents from the field. But his regiment became separated during the charge, and then he often forgot about the battle and chased the enemy for miles.

Cromwell was as brave as Prince Rupert but his troops were better disciplined. They advanced at a trot. So when Cromwell defeated the enemy cavalry, he was able to swing round and crush the enemy infantry. The difference between Rupert and Cromwell helps to explain why Parliament won the Civil War.

Cavalry
Cavalry troopers fought on horseback using swords and pistols. They rarely wore armour, but for protection they wore a 'buff' coat made of thick leather.

Musketeers

This sequence of pictures shows how to load and fire a musket.

The musketeer cleans and prepares the flintlock firing mechanism (pictures 1 and 2), rams home the gunpowder and the bullet (3), and finally mounts and fires the musket (4 and 5).

Muskets were only accurate at short range. Musketeers poured the charges of gunpowder into wooden cases before a battle, and hung the cases on a strap called a bandolier. Musketeers also carried swords.

Pikemen

Because it took a long time to load a musket, the musketeers needed to be protected from enemy attacks.

While the musketeers were re-loading, therefore, the pikemen would move in front of them and level their pikes. Pikemen also carried swords for close fighting.

This detail from the picture of the battle of Naseby overleaf shows pikemen and musketeers lined up together.

The King's

Broad Moor

Cavaliers

The King's
Reg.t
or Life

Prince Rupert
Prince Maurice
S.r Barnard Astley

His Tertia

Col.t

K: Charles I.

Left Wing Commanded
by Commiss.r General Ireton

Col.l Harmadeth
Reg.t Commanded by Major
Huntington

Col.l Reg.t Commiss.r Gen.l Ireton

Major Gen.t

Reg.t Col.l Fleetwoods Reg.t Troops of Horse

Forlorn
Hope Musquetiers

S.r Hardres Waller

Coll D.

Coll Pride
Reserve

Mill Hill

L.t Coll Prides
Rear Guard

The Train Guarded by Fire-locks

60

The battle of Naseby (1645)

Use your knowledge of Civil War warfare to help you find:

- the king;
- the king's army, with Rupert's cavalry on its right flank;
- Parliament's army, with the cavalry commanded by Cromwell and by Ireton (another Parliamentary general) on the flanks;
- the troops of pikemen and musketeers in the centre;
- the artillery (cannons);
- the king's baggage on Broad Moor, and Parliament's baggage on Mill Hill, guarded with muskets;
- the village of Naseby;
- villagers who have come out to watch.

The Execution

The army had promised to bring 'that man of blood' to account – and they did. On 30 January 1649, Charles was executed.

A modern textbook gives this account of the execution:

A   Execution in Whitehall

1   On Tuesday, 30 January 1649, Charles I was brought to his own Banqueting Hall in Whitehall, London.

2   It was a gloomy, cold day, white with frost and snow.

3   A troop of soldiers . . . surrounded the black-draped scaffold set in front of the building . . . to prevent any attempt at rescue.

4   Dense crowds surged forward, stretching their necks to see him and calling out prayers and blessings.

5   The scaffold itself was packed with officers and clergy.

6   Charles's executioners were disguised by cloaks, masks and obviously false hair and beards.

7   Charles then stripped off his jewels and his outer clothing.

8   The block was only ten inches high so he had to lie flat to place his head on it.

9   After a few seconds, he gave a signal to the executioner.

10   The axe swung down, cutting off his head at one blow.

11   An eyewitness wrote of this moment: 'There was such a groan by the thousands then present, as I never heard before and desire I may never hear again.'

L.E. Snellgrove, *The Early Modern Age (1972)*

B   A Dutch engraving from the time, showing the execution of the king.

C   A Royalist painting showing the execution of the king. The main picture shows Charles taking off his cloak, then being beheaded. The side pictures show Charles, the procession to the scaffold, the executioner with the head, and people dipping handkerchiefs in the blood.

An Everlasting Blot?

The Irish rebelled in 1641. The Irish Catholics killed many Protestants.
In 1649, after Charles I's execution, Cromwell went to Ireland. The first town he attacked was Drogheda.

1 The capture of Drogheda

I asked the governor to surrender, but I got no satisfactory answer . . . .

The guns opened two good gaps in the wall. About five o'clock in the evening, we began the attack . . . and after a very hot battle they gave ground.

The enemy retreated into the Mill-Mount, a place very strong . . . and being in the heat of action, I forbade our men to spare any that were in arms in the town, and, I think, that night we put to the sword about 2,000 men . . . .

The next day, the two towers were summoned to surrender; but they refused. From one of the towers, they killed and wounded some of our men – when they submitted, every tenth man of the soldiers was killed. The soldiers in the other tower were all spared.

This is a judgement of God upon these barbarous wretches, who have dipped their hands in so much innocent blood; and it will stop the shedding of much blood in the future. These are the satisfactory excuses for my actions, which otherwise must give much sadness and regret.

Letter from **Oliver Cromwell** *to the House of Commons,*
17 September 1649.

to spare: *to spare their lives – not to kill them.*
any that were in arms: *Irish soldiers who continued to fight against Cromwell's men.*
dipped their hands in innocent blood: *Cromwell blamed Irish Catholics for the deaths of the Protestants in the Irish Rebellion of 1641.*

Cromwell's men attack Drogheda – a picture from the time.

Hero or Villain?

Over the years, historians have written many different things about Cromwell's victory at Drogheda.

2 Cromwell promised to spare the lives of any who would lay down their weapons . . . but when they had surrendered, the order 'No quarter' went round.

Letter from the **Marquis of Ormond**, *1649.*
Ormond was one of the Irish leaders, but he was not present at Drogheda.

quarter: *in the seventeenth century an army would sometimes give its enemies 'quarter' (they would not kill them). At Drogheda, however, Cromwell did not give quarter.*

3 His famous victories in Ireland . . . have crowned him in the opinion of all the world as one of the wisest and most successful leaders of all time.

Mercurius Politicus (3 June 1650), a newspaper published by the government.

4 At least 3,000, besides women and children, were put to the sword.

Anthony Wood, *1674.*
Wood was the brother of a soldier in Cromwell's army.

5 It is possible that, in such a scene, women and children may have been accidentally killed; but there is no evidence of it from any eyewitness, only general rumours.

The Irish rebellion had cost nearly 600,000 lives. It was necessary to end such horrible scenes, and to end them swiftly.

J.A. Froude, *The English in Ireland (1881)*

6 The laws of war allowed him to do this, for he had given them a chance to surrender and they had refused it.

M. Elliot, *Tudors and Stuarts (1961).*
This book was written by an English historian.

7 His upbringing had made him fear and hate Roman Catholics . . . . He had heard tales of massacres of Protestants in Ireland, and had come to regard the Irish as beyond forgiveness. Cromwell's cruelty in Ireland is an everlasting blot on the name of a great man.

R.J. Unstead, *Crown and Parliament (1975)*

8 Cromwell lost his self-control at Drogheda . . . . In the heat of the moment occurred the incident that has blackened Oliver Cromwell's name down history for 300 years.

Antonia Fraser, *Cromwell (1973)*

65

Women in War

When the Civil War started, Margaret Eure wrote: 'All that women can do is to pray for better times.' Women were thought to be 'the weaker vessel' – weaker, gentler and less intelligent than men. The war changed all that. In 1645, the poet James Strong wrote: 'To most it's known, the weaker vessels are stronger grown.'

The information on these two pages will tell you about women in the Civil War.

1 Lady Lucy Hutchinson nursed wounded soldiers of both sides. She was not frightened when a Roundhead captain complained that she was helping Royalists. She told him that 'she had done nothing but her duty, in humanity to them'.

2 In many towns, women raised money for the army. The women were called 'Maiden troops'.

3 When Charles I was in prison after the war, Jane Whorwood carried messages and money to him. She also smuggled acid to him to dissolve the bars of his cell. When Charles was executed, Jane was one of the few who dared to cheer for him.

4 Some women, like 'Mr Clarke' (below), dressed themselves in men's clothes and joined the army. 'Mr Clarke' fired a musket, wrestled, drank and smoked like the other soldiers, and was only discovered when 'he' gave birth to a baby boy!

5 Elizabeth Alkin acted as a nurse and a spy and wrote pamphlets supporting Parliament.

6 During the siege of Nottingham in 1643, while the men fought, women walked round looking for fires to put out.

7 In 1643, during the siege of Lyme in Dorset, the women of the town threw rocks at the attackers and filled the defenders' cartridges with gunpowder. One woman lost her hand during the siege, but she said: 'I am glad that I had a hand to lose for Jesus Christ, and am willing to lose my life also.'

8 During the siege of Gloucester in 1644, women helped to build the earth mounds to defend the town.

9 Lady Cholmley helped her husband during the siege of Scarborough Castle in 1644. She tended the wounded while he defended the castle. He said that 'though by nature timid, she showed a courage above her sex'.

10 After the war, in 1649, women presented *The Petition of Women* to Parliament. It demanded 'rights and freedom . . . and a share in the government'. When they were told to 'stay home and wash the dishes', they said that the war had left them no dishes to wash.

11 In 1643, more than six thousand women marched to the House of Commons to ask Parliament to make peace with the king. They were driven away by soldiers. Some were killed.

13 In 1645, Charlotte, Countess of Derby, defended Lathom House in Derbyshire so fiercely that people said she had 'stolen her husband's trousers'.

14 Women had to cope when their husbands left home to join the army. 'I am a lone woman,' complained one wife. Another wrote to her soldier husband: 'Why can everyone come home except you?'

15 Many women had to suffer the horrors of war. Alice Stonier of Staffordshire and her five children were robbed and their house was burned down. Her husband Thomas was 'pressed' into the army – and killed almost immediately. The family ended up sleeping in the fields.

12 Mary, Lady Bankes, defended Corfe Castle in Dorset for most of the war. Helped by her daughters, her maids and five soldiers, she dropped stones and hot ashes on the enemy as they climbed their scaling ladders.

The World Turned Upside Down

The Civil War and the execution of the king broke down the normal controls in society. People felt free to think and speak as they liked. If Parliament could overthrow the king and the bishops, why should they obey the lord of the manor and the vicar? Many different 'sects' grew up with all sorts of ideas.

Quakers

Quakers (above) refused to have ministers. At their church meetings, anybody could speak. Sometimes they became so filled with the Holy Spirit that they shook all over.

Quakers never took their hats off to their 'betters'.

There were about thirty-five thousand Quakers by 1660. Their founder was George Fox, but many of their leaders were women.

Diggers

The Diggers were the first communists. Their leader was Gerrard Winstanley. They believed that all men and women were equal, and had an equal right to the land. They moved onto the Common at Walton-on-Thames, in Surrey, and farmed it together. They did not allow any private property or possessions.

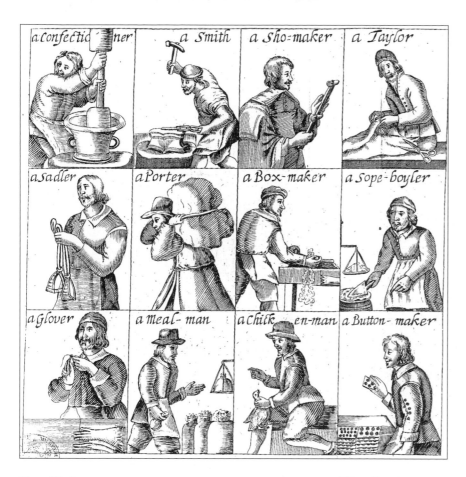

a Confectidner   a Smith   a Sho-maker   a Taylor

a Sadler   a Porter   a Box-maker   a Sope-boyler

a Glover   a Meal-man   a Chilk-en-man   a Button-maker

Levellers

The Levellers wanted a new, fairer society – even for ordinary people such as chicken-men and button-makers (left).

They wanted elections every year, at which all men over 21 would vote. They wanted freedom of speech, freedom of worship and better education for everyone. They believed that men and women were equal.

The Levellers' leader was John Lilburne.

Familists

Familists belonged to a sect called the Family of Love. They did not believe in heaven or hell. They said that Christ was just a good man who set an example for people to follow.

Familists claimed that they did not have to obey the laws of the country, and said that one day they would conquer the world.

Many of their leaders were women.

The Ranters

The Ranters (below) believed that, as Christ had died for their sins, Christians could behave as they wanted. Drunkenness, adultery, theft and murder were not sinful. In fact, it was good to sin.

One of the Ranters' leaders, John Robson, claimed that he could raise the dead. His followers said that he was God, his wife was the Virgin Mary, and his son was Jesus Christ.

Fifth Monarchists

The Fifth Monarchists believed that the death of Charles I had opened the way for a new government: the 'fifth monarchy' (the reign of Christ on earth).

The Fifth Monarchists were mostly soldiers and poor townspeople. They believed that Christ was going to return and set up a perfect world in which poor people would make the laws. There would be no more disease or pain. They also believed that this new kingdom would be brought in by violence, and they rebelled in 1657 and 1661.

Their leader was Thomas Venner. Many of their prophets were women.

A KINGDOM UNITED

Oliver Cromwell

In January 1649, after the execution of Charles I, England became a republic (a country without a monarch) for the only time in its history. It was called the Commonwealth, because it wanted the 'weal' (the good) of the community.

The Rump

The Long Parliament had been sitting since 1640. Some MPs had died. 5
The army had expelled all those MPs who supported Charles I. By 1649 only fifty MPs were left attending Parliament. They were called the 10 'Rump' Parliament.
The REAL power in the land was the army and its leader, Oliver Cromwell. In April 1653 15 he went to the House of Commons with a group of soldiers and drove the MPs out.

The Barebones Parliament

Oliver Cromwell became the 20 real ruler of England. He wanted the people to rule through Parliament, but he could not find a Parliament which would rule in the way he wanted it to! 25
Cromwell asked all the Puritan churches to send him the names of 'godly men'. From these lists, in July 1653, he chose 140 'saints' to make up a Parliament. The first name on the list was that of Praisegod Barebones, so the Parliament became known as the 'Barebones' 30 Parliament. It was a failure. The saints spent all their time arguing. On 12 December 1653 the Barebones Parliament abolished itself.

The Protectorate

On 16 December 1653 a group of army officers published a document called *The Instrument of Government*. It asked Cromwell to be the 'Lord Protector' of England.

Cromwell believed that he had been called by God to be Lord Protector. He still tried to rule with a Parliament. A first Parliament met in September 1654, and a second in September 1656. However, some MPs tried to reduce his power, so Cromwell dismissed both Parliaments. Yet, when the MPs asked him to become king, he refused this also.

In August 1655, Cromwell divided the country into eleven districts. Each was controlled by a Major General and a force of soldiers. To pay for these forces, Cromwell collected an illegal tax from the Royalists. When some judges opposed him, he put them in prison.

The Major Generals imposed a strict Puritan rule in England. Bear-baiting, cockfighting, the theatre, Sunday trading, horse-racing, playing cards, football and wrestling were all banned. Ale-houses were closed and drunkenness was punished. Offenders were put in the stocks or imprisoned. Maypoles were chopped down because the Puritans disapproved of dancing.

Cromwell and the Major Generals were hated. The Protectorate was really a military dictatorship, kept in power by an army of fifty thousand soldiers, but it kept the peace in a country that had been at war for nearly ten years. During these years, Jews were allowed to live in England (for the first time since 1290), and Cromwell allowed people to worship freely in private. He abolished out-of-date laws, and reduced the number of crimes which carried the death penalty.

Foreign policy

Cromwell's foreign policy was very successful. He built up a strong navy. He went to war with Spain, and in May 1655 the navy captured Jamaica in the West Indies. It is sometimes said that he laid the foundations of the British Empire.

Oliver Cromwell died in 1658.

In this woodcut from the time, a Puritan (on the left) criticises Christmas. In 1652 Parliament passed a law forbidding people to celebrate Christmas Day. Troops burst into people's houses and took away their Christmas dinners.

Restoration and Revolution

In April 1660, Parliament asked Charles II, the son of Charles I, to return to England from exile to become king. This is called the
5 Restoration.

The actress Nell Gwyn, Charles II's mistress. After the hated 'rule of the saints', Charles's reign was a time of fun and
10 naughty behaviour. The theatres became very popular. But it
15 was also a time when science, writing and art flourished.

Charles II

Like his father, Charles II did not like
20 ruling with a Parliament. In 1670, he secretly promised King Louis XIV of France that he would make England a Roman Catholic country.

Parliament was loyal to Charles, but it
25 was determined that England should stay Protestant. In 1678, a trickster called Titus Oates published the names of 102 Catholics who, he said, were plotting to massacre the Protestants.
30 Although it was all complete nonsense, the 'Popish Plot' caused panic in London. Protestants carried clubs in case a Catholic tried to murder them. A dozen Catholics were executed.
35 Charles's brother, James, the heir to the throne, was a Roman Catholic.

Some people tried to force Charles to promise that James would never succeed to the throne. They were nicknamed 'Whigs', after some Scottish rebels. 40 People who supported Charles and James were nicknamed 'Tories', after some Catholic bandits who hid in the bogs of Ireland. The Whigs and the Tories were the first political parties 45 in England.

James II

After 1681, the excitement of the Popish Plot died down. When Charles died in 1685, James II succeeded to the throne.

James was openly Roman Catholic. 50 He allowed Roman Catholics to worship freely. Judges who disagreed with him were thrown into prison. James began to build up a permanent ('standing') army.

People were alarmed, but they knew 55 that James would die soon, and they thought that he would be succeeded by his daughter Mary, a Protestant.

The first years of Charles II's reign were years of disaster. In 1665 the plague killed a fifth of the population of London. In 1666 the Great Fire of London (left) destroyed the city.

The Glorious Revolution

In 1688, however, James's wife gave birth to a boy. English Protestants were horrified. A group of seven leading politicians invited William of Orange – Mary's husband and leader of the Dutch army – to come to England to be king.

William arrived in England in November 1688. Only a few English people supported James; they were called Jacobites (the Latin word for James is Jacobus). James fled to France.

William had not inherited the throne. He had been given the crown by Parliament. In return, he agreed to the Bill of Rights (see below).

In 1701, the Act of Settlement was passed, stating that a Catholic could never be king or queen of England. When Queen Anne died in 1714, the throne passed to a German – George of Hanover. The English people had decided that they wanted a 'constitutional monarchy'.

William and Mary agreed to the Bill of Rights (1689). They promised to obey the law and to call frequent Parliaments. They promised not to keep a standing army, and gave Parliament the right to appoint the judges. Parliament also made sure that it controlled William's money. It gave him a small annual payment called the 'civil list', to support his household. If William wanted any more money, he had to go to Parliament to ask for it.

This kind of 'rule with limits' is called 'constitutional monarchy'.

Ireland

After 1649, Cromwell took away the land of every Irishman who had not supported the English Parliament. He gave the land to his soldiers as payment.

5 Catholics who lost their land were 'transplanted' to live on poor land in the west of Ireland. Many abandoned their children. The Government sold the orphans to slave traders, who took them 10 to Jamaica. When the supply of orphans ran out, the traders started kidnapping Irish children – just as they would kidnap Africans in the next century.

Most of Ireland's land was now owned 15 by English Protestants. Many of these chose to be absentee landlords, who lived in England. They were often bad landlords, who cared for nothing except getting the rent out of the tenants.

20 When the English threw out James II, the Irish rebelled.

The 1689 rebellion failed, however. James was defeated at the Battle of the Boyne (1 July 1690).

The English Parliament passed laws to 25 punish the Irish. Catholics were not allowed to vote, or to be MPs. No Catholic was allowed to be a teacher, to sell books, or to own a gun.

Catholics could not own a horse worth 30 £5 or more. If a Protestant offered £5 for a Catholic's horse, he could take it away without paying.

Worst of all, a Catholic could not leave his land to his eldest child when 35 he died. It had to be divided between all of his children. This meant that the Catholics' farms got smaller every generation, until they were too tiny to feed a family. 40

The Irish were forbidden to export their cattle, milk and butter to England. Irish agriculture and industry collapsed.

These laws made Ireland poor.

The Jacobites and the '45 Rebellion

Until the eighteenth century, Scotland was an independent country with its own Parliament. By the Act of 5 Union (1707), however, England and Scotland became a United Kingdom. Many Scots hated the Union.

After the Glorious Revolution 10 of 1688, James II had gone to live in France. Those Scots who hated the Union hoped that they could break free from England if the Stuart kings 15 returned. They were Jacobites.

In 1715, there was a small Jacobite rebellion in Scotland, but it failed.

Bonnie Prince Charlie

The years 1715-45 were years 20 of peace and prosperity. People became richer and happier.

In 1745, the king of England was King George II. Many people had forgotten about the 25 Stuart kings.

But the Stuarts had not forgotten. Charles Edward Stuart was the grandson of James II. In 1745, he left 30 France and went to Scotland to claim his crown. Many Scots joined him. Most of them – 'the Highlanders' – came from the Highlands in the far 35 north of Scotland.

Charles invaded England. He got as far as Derby, but then he turned back. The English army chased him back to Scotland, where it defeated him at the battle of Culloden.

Charles had to run away. For months, he 40 was on the run in the Highlands. In the end, he escaped to France. But he never came back to Scotland again. He took to drink and died in 1788.

A map of the '45 Rebellion.

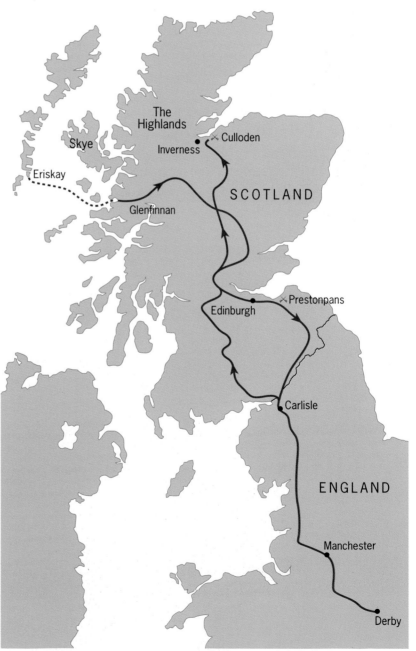

KEY
—— Prince Charles's route

75

The Story of the '45 Rebellion

1 Charles Edward Stuart landed in Scotland on the island of Eriskay on 23 July 1745. He had just seven men with him.

2 Charles raised his standard at Glenfinnan on 19 August 1745. Hundreds of Highlanders joined him. They met an English army under General John Cope at the battle of Prestonpans on 21 September 1745. It lasted four minutes. The Highlanders made a mad rush at the English soldiers . . . who ran away! The Scots killed 300 and captured 1,500 English soldiers.

3 By the end of September, Charles had 5,000 men in his army. He marched south, capturing Edinburgh, Carlisle and Manchester. In London, there was panic. It seemed that nothing could stop Charles. People were sure that he was going to conquer England.

But no Englishmen joined Charles's army, and the Scottish clan leaders began to argue amongst themselves.

4 At Derby – only 100 miles from London – the Scots refused to go any further. Charles turned around on 6 December 1745, and marched back to Scotland. He was chased by a large English army of 18,000 men, led by the Duke of Cumberland. This humorous picture shows the English army setting off. Many of Charles's soldiers deserted and went back home.

5 At Culloden, in the north of Scotland, Charles had only 2,000 men. He tried a surprise night attack on the English army, but he set off too late. His men arrived tired and hungry, just in time to see the English army waking up and getting ready to fight.

The battle took place on 16 April 1746. For 20 minutes the English cannons bombarded the Scots. The Scots charged, but the English army destroyed them. Half the Highlanders were killed. The Duke of Cumberland (on the white horse in the foreground) was very cruel.

6 Charles spent several months being hunted by Cumberland's soldiers. He had many narrow escapes, but no one betrayed him to the English. In the end, he went back to France.

The Scottish Jacobites loved 'Bonnie Prince Charlie'. They made up songs about him which have never been forgotten – songs such as *Charlie is my darling*, *Over the sea to Skye* and *Will ye no come back again?*

Why Did Charles Turn Back?

Charles had marched as far as Derby in England, then turned back. Sources 7–10 suggest different reasons why he did this.

This portrait of Bonnie Prince Charlie was painted between 1739 and 1745. Look at it and suggest reasons why he failed to win back the crown in 1745.

7 By the time Charles reached Derby, the trap was closing on him. A British army had been brought back from the Continent, another had followed him from Scotland, while thousands of citizens were arming themselves to defend London. Charles turned back.

L.E. Snellgrove, *The Making of the United Kingdom (1993)*

9 In December, they reached Derby. Here the Scottish chiefs gloomily refused to go any further. Their own men were weary and footsore; many had deserted . . . .

In vain, Charles begged them to continue, but on the next day, 'Black Friday', he was forced to agree to the retreat.

R.J. Unstead, *Great People of Modern Times (1956)*

8 Charles led the Highlanders as far as Derby. But no English people of any importance joined him. He still wanted to push on, but his officers persuaded him to march back to Scotland.

Joe Scott, *The Making of the United Kingdom (1993)*

10 The increased prosperity of the Scots helps to explain the failure of the Jacobite rebellion of 1745. There was little support and although Charles's army reached Derby in England, it found no support and retreated.

James Mason, *The Making of the United Kingdom (1993)*

??? QUESTION ???

What different reasons do sources 7–10 give as to why Charles turned back?

INDEX